200
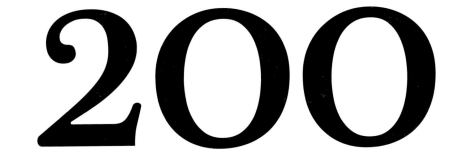

PICNIC & TAILGATE
RECIPES

CAROL BECKERMAN

SELLERS
PUBLISHING

A Quintet Book

Published by Sellers Publishing, Inc.
161 John Roberts Road, South Portland, Maine 04106
Visit our Web site: www.sellerspublishing.com
E-mail: rsp@rsvp.com

ISBN: 978-1-4162-4542-1
Library of Congress Control Number: 2014950214
QTT.RFPT

This book was conceived, designed and produced by
Quintet Publishing Limited
4th Floor, Sheridan House
114-116 Western Road
Hove, East Sussex
BN3 1DD

Project Editor: Ella Lines
Photographer: Tony Briscoe
Food Stylist: Julia Azarello
Designer: Rod Teasdale
Art Director: Michael Charles
Editorial Director: Emma Bastow
Publisher: Mark Searle

10 9 8 7 6 5 4 3 2 1

Printed in China by Toppan Leefung

CONTENTS

introduction

tips for outdoor picnic events and cooking

- Good planning in advance is essential.

- Skewer and marinate kebabs, and shape and pack burger patties between sheets of wax paper the night before. Slice and pack up burger toppings the night before, too.

- For a posh picnic, pack real dishes and pretty glasses. Candles in glass jars or even candelabra at a champagne picnic are a good idea when darkness falls.

- Do not forget something to sit on. Folding chairs are ideal but a rug with a waterproof base, is a good idea too. Take a helium balloon to float on a long string from your car so that friends can find you.

- Games are a great idea, so plan which ones to bring.

- Gas barbecues are very popular now, as they are so easy to use. They are quick to fire up, there is no need to wait while the charcoal gets going, and small bottles of gas are easily obtainable to make transportation easy.

- Get to the designated parking lot early for a concert picnic or tailgating event. Check the venue's rules with concern to alcohol or glass. Use containers to keep everything in the right place. All dry items such as plates, napkins, and utensils can be carried in plastic bins. Do not forget bottle openers, garbage bags, ice, water, sun protection, and small plastic bags for taking home leftovers.

- Keep all cold and cooked foods in a cooler or thermal tray to keep them at a safe temperature. Perishables like meats should go into one cooler, and vegetables and drinks should go into a separate cooler.

- Make sure your team's colors are easily visible; color-keyed food, such as cupcakes with frosting in your team's colors, will help you get into conversation with other fans.

- Plan to have enough time to clean and store everything back into the vehicles after the party. Or you could even carry on your tailgating party after the game finishes, so that you are still rocking while everyone else is struggling to exit the parking lot. When you are ready to leave, ensure the grill is extinguished properly.

food & drink suggestions

- Barbecued steak, chicken, hot dogs, sausages, hamburgers, and kebabs.

- Buffalo wings, subs, dips, corn chips, nachos, and pretzels.

- Potato salad, coleslaw, bean salads, and other salads.

- Treats for the children, such as shaped sandwiches, cookies and cupcakes, and sliced fresh fruit for dipping.

- Cook or bake ahead—items such as baked potatoes will benefit from being cooked ahead of time, and only need to be heated up rather than cooked on the day.

- Soda, juice, and water are essential. Label your coolers so that guests can find drinks easily. Freeze water bottles to use in coolers so that you have cold water to drink after they melt. In colder weather, use thermos flasks to keep coffee, cocoa, or mulled cider or wine hot.

- Everybody in the parking lot will have ribs, chicken, hamburgers, and hot dogs. If you want to get people's attention, try the recipes in this book.

checklist

- Tickets for the game or venue.

- Food, drink, ice, and coolers.

- Grill, charcoal, matches or lighter, grilling tools and utensils, camping stove, pots and pans for cooking, oven mitts and apron, cutting board, serving tray.

- Folding table and chairs, table cloth and blankets or rugs.

- Canopy, team flag, themed decorations, and games.

- Plates, glasses and flat wear—real, paper, or plastic, candles and candelabra.

- Sunscreen, first aid kit, fire extinguisher, and hand sanitizer.

- CD or MP3 player, ipod, portable speakers, music.

- Portable power, generator, kerosene heater or fan.

- Binoculars, camera, rain gear, umbrellas.

- Tailgating couch, outdoor TV, self cranking radio.

- Clean-up supplies, garbage bags, Ziploc bags.

starters &
light bites

Get your picnic or tailgating party off to the right start with these little appetizers that you can enjoy before the main event — they will tickle your taste buds and get you in the mood for a celebratory feast.

crab cakes

A great favorite with everyone, these crab cakes freeze well before cooking, so double up the recipe and put some away for another day.

1 lb. crabmeat, thawed if frozen
1 clove garlic, minced
½ red medium bell pepper, finely chopped
2 scallions, finely chopped
2 tbsp. chopped fresh parsley
2 tbsp. mayonnaise
1 tbsp. Dijon mustard
zest of 1 lemon
½ tsp. paprika
½ tsp. salt
freshly ground black pepper
2 eggs, lightly beaten
½ cup/2 ½ oz. breadcrumbs
2–4 tbsp. unsalted butter
Makes 12

In a bowl, combine the crabmeat, garlic, bell pepper, scallions, parsley, mayonnaise, mustard, lemon zest, paprika, salt, and several grindings of black pepper. Stir in the eggs, then mix in half of the breadcrumbs using clean hands or a wooden spoon.

Form the mixture into approximately 12 crab cakes. Put the remaining breadcrumbs in a shallow dish and then dredge the crab cakes in the breadcrumbs.

Heat 2 tablespoons butter in a skillet and cook half of the crab cakes over medium heat for 3–4 minutes each side, or until golden brown. Repeat with the remaining crab cakes, adding more butter to the skillet as needed.

Serve the cooked crab cakes with fresh tomato and red onion salsa (see page 25).

NOW TRY THIS

ginger crab cakes
Peel and mince a 1-inch piece of fresh ginger root and add to the crabmeat with ¼ teaspoon Tabasco sauce.

crab & shrimp cakes
Replace half the crabmeat with 8 ounces of raw, prepared shrimp, chopped into small pieces.

fish cakes
Replace the crabmeat with cooked and flaked white fish, such as cod or tilapia, or salmon. Add a few finely chopped shrimp, if desired.

crab cake canapés
Halve the size of the crab cakes. Lightly mash some salsa and put ½ teaspoon on top of each cake. Garnish with a tiny sprig of parsley.

shrimp with garlic & smoked paprika

This recipe encapsulates the simplicity of rustic Spanish cooking. The mingling flavors of the marinade combine beautifully with the sweet succulent shrimp, while charred edges from the barbecue or grill give the slightest of crunches and a heady smoked aroma.

4 large shrimp, heads off, deveined, but shells on

1 tsp. sea salt

3 cloves garlic, finely chopped

½ tsp. smoked paprika

2 tbsp. olive oil

zest and juice of 1 lemon

Serves 4

Place the shrimp in a bowl with the salt, garlic, paprika, olive oil, and lemon zest. Mix, then let marinate for 15 minutes.

Heat a griddle pan or barbecue grill on high until it begins to smoke. Lay the shrimp on the pan or grill and cook for 2–3 minutes on each side until charred on the outside but nice and opaque in the middle. Sprinkle with the lemon juice in the last minute of cooking. Transfer to a serving dish and eat with your fingers.

NOW TRY THIS

shrimp with garlic, cilantro & lemongrass
Replace the paprika in the marinade with 1 tablespoon chopped fresh cilantro and a 1-inch piece of lemongrass, chopped finely.

shrimp with garlic & peppercorns
Replace the paprika and lemon zest with 1 ½ teaspoons crushed pink peppercorns.

shrimp with garlic, smoked paprika & chile
Add 1 chopped small red chile to the marinade.

shrimp with garlic, ginger, chile & cilantro
Replace the paprika and lemon zest in the marinade with 1 teaspoon grated fresh ginger root, 1 chopped green chile, and 1 tablespoon chopped fresh cilantro.

chipotle popcorn chicken

Quick and easy to prepare, these little chicken bites are marinated in buttermilk overnight, and are equally good served warm or cold.

4 chicken breasts

1 ½ cups/12 fl. oz. buttermilk, plus 2 tbsp.

1 cup/6 oz. canned chipotle peppers, finely chopped

2 cups/9 oz. all-purpose flour

1 tsp. paprika

1 tsp. garlic powder

1 tsp. onion powder

1 tsp. cayenne pepper

1 tsp. dried oregano

1 tbsp. freshly chopped parsley

2 eggs, beaten

canola oil for deep-frying

4 tbsp. freshly chopped cilantro

salt and freshly ground black pepper

Serves 8

Cut the chicken into 1 ½-inch pieces. Place in a bowl, cover with buttermilk, and add the chopped chipotle peppers. Cover and place in the refrigerator for anything from one hour to overnight.

Drain the chicken from the buttermilk. Place the flour in a large bowl, and add the paprika, garlic and onion powders, cayenne pepper, oregano, and parsley, and plenty of salt and freshly ground black pepper. In a shallow bowl, whisk the eggs with 2 tablespoons buttermilk. Dredge each piece of chicken in the seasoned flour, then dip each piece of chicken in the beaten egg, letting the excess drip off, and dredge in the flour again, making sure that each piece is well coated.

In a large pan, over a medium-high heat, place enough oil to come half way up the sides, and using a thermometer, heat until it reaches 350°F. Deep-fry the chicken in batches for about 3 minutes each side, or until golden brown and cooked through. Drain on paper towels, and when cold, store in the refrigerator until required. To serve, sprinkle with the freshly chopped cilantro, and a little extra salt.

NOW TRY THIS

with ranch dip
Mix together ½ cup/4 fluid ounces buttermilk, 2 tablespoons sour cream, 1 tablespoon mayo, ½ teaspoon chopped parsley, 1 minced clove garlic, and ½ teaspoon Dijon mustard.

with honey mustard dip
Mix ¾ cup/6 fluid ounces sour cream, 4 tablespoons mayo, and 4 tablespoons Dijon mustard. Mix 4 tablespoons honey with 1 tablespoon lemon juice, add to sour cream, and whisk until smooth.

with blue cheese dip
Mix together 4 tablespoons each of buttermilk, sour cream, and crumbled blue cheese. Add 1 crushed clove garlic, ¼ teaspoon each sweet paprika and salt, and mix until combined.

grilled calamari with garlic & paprika

It is important in this recipe that the pan is exceptionally hot so the squid is quickly cooked to tender perfection. Squid must always be cooked very fast over high heat or slowly over a long period, otherwise the result is a chewy, rubberlike disaster.

1 large squid (about ½ lb.), membrane and sac removed

½ tsp. sea salt

3 cloves garlic, finely chopped

zest of 1 orange

½ tsp. hot smoked paprika

2 tbsp. olive oil

Serves 4

Open up the squid by cutting along the side seam. Wash and dry thoroughly. Very gently, with the tip of a sharp knife, score the squid in a crisscross pattern. Cut into 4 pieces. Place the squid in a bowl with the salt, garlic, orange zest, paprika, and olive oil. Let marinate for 5 minutes.

Heat a grill over a high heat until it is smoking, and then lay the pieces of squid on the griddle (I like to weigh them down to stop them from curling up, using something heavy like another pan.) Cook for 1–2 minutes on each side. Cut into 2 ½-inch diamonds and place on a serving plate.

NOW TRY THIS

spicy calamari with garlic & lemongrass
Replace the orange zest and paprika with ½ teaspoon dried red pepper flakes and a ½-inch piece of lemongrass, finely chopped.

calamari with garlic & lemon thyme
Replace the orange zest and paprika with 1 teaspoon chopped fresh lemon thyme. Squeeze over the juice of half a lemon before serving.

spicy calamari with garlic, lemon & mint
Replace the orange zest and smoked paprika with the zest of 1 lemon, 1 tablespoon chopped red chiles, 1 finely chopped scallion, and 1 tablespoon chopped fresh mint.

monkfish with garlic & smoked paprika
Replace the squid with 7 ounces monkfish cut into ½-inch slices.

mushroom tart with gruyere & pine nuts

Served with a green salad, this tart makes a lovely lunch or light supper.

1 x 11 oz. ready-to-bake shortcrust pastry sheet

1 large egg, lightly beaten

1 head of garlic, unpeeled

½ cup/4 oz. ricotta cheese

4 tbsp. crème fraîche or sour cream

2 tbsp. salted butter

1 tbsp. olive oil

1 ½ lb. mixed mushrooms, such as oyster, chanterelle, shiitake, and portobello

¾ cups/4 oz. grated Gruyère

1 oz. pine nuts

salt and freshly ground black pepper

Serves 4–6

Preheat the oven to 400°F. Unroll the pastry on a lightly floured surface and use to line a 9-inch tart pan. Bake blind for 15 minutes. Remove from the oven, prick the surface with a fork, and brush the surface with lightly beaten egg. Then bake for 10 minutes more. Transfer to a wire rack to cool.

Boil the garlic head in a saucepan filled with water for 15 minutes, then drain. When cool enough to handle, pop the garlic cloves out of their skins and mash in a bowl with the ricotta and crème fraîche until smooth. Season with salt and pepper.

Heat the butter and olive oil in a skillet and sauté the mushrooms for 10–15 minutes, until they are tender and any liquid has evaporated. Season with salt and pepper. To assemble, spread the ricotta and garlic mixture over the base of the cooled tart shell. Layer half of the mushroom mixture, then half of the grated Gruyère. Repeat the mushroom and Gruyère layers and sprinkle the pine nuts over the cheese. Bake for 25 minutes, or until the filling is hot and the pine nuts are golden brown.

NOW TRY THIS

mushroom tart with thyme
Add 2 teaspoons of chopped fresh thyme leaves to the mushrooms as they are frying.

mushroom & onion tart
Add 1 small red onion, sliced, to the mushrooms in the skillet.

mushroom tart on puff pastry
Replace the shortcrust with ready-to-bake puff pastry. Roll out to a 13 x 9-inch rectangle. Using a sharp knife, score a rectangular border, ¼ inch from the edge of the pastry, taking care not to touch the bottom with the knife. Glaze the border with a lightly beaten egg. Do not prebake the puff pastry; simply fill and bake for 25 minutes.

bacon wrapped pineapple

These pineapple chunks are wrapped in bacon and cooked until crispy in a light and sweet but spicy sauce.

8 slices premium smoked bacon
20-oz. can pineapple chunks, well drained
½ cup/3 ½ oz. brown sugar
8 tbsp. mayonnaise
4 tbsp. tomato ketchup
½ tsp. hot chili powder
½ tsp. crushed red pepper flakes
½ tsp. ground cumin
salt and freshly ground black pepper

Makes 24

Pre-heat the oven to 350°F. Cut each slice of bacon into three and wrap each one round a pineapple chunk. Secure with a toothpick, and place in a well greased shallow baking pan.

In a small bowl, mix together the brown sugar, mayonnaise, tomato ketchup, chili powder, crushed pepper flakes, ground cumin, and salt and freshly ground black pepper.

Pour the sauce over the bacon and pineapple, and place the pan on the grill for about 15 minutes, or until the bacon is crispy and the sauce has reduced slightly. Turn the bacon rolls over a couple of times. Keep warm until serving.

NOW TRY THIS

bacon wrapped shrimp
Use large shrimp in place of the pineapple.

bacon wrapped sausages
Omit the pineapple and all the rest of the ingredients except the bacon. Cut 12 cocktail sausages in half and each bacon slice in three. Wrap one piece of bacon around each sausage half and grill as before.

bacon wrapped prunes
Omit the pineapple and all the rest of the ingredients except the bacon. Cut each bacon slice in half. Stone 16 soft dried prunes, and stuff a little mango chutney inside each one. Wrap one piece of bacon around each prune, and grill as before.

sausage rolls with salsa

These sausage rolls are a little spicy with lots of black pepper, ideal to enjoy with either a glass of beer or homemade soda.

1 clove garlic, minced

4 tbsp. freshly chopped parsley

2 tsp. dried sage

2 tsp. cayenne pepper

1 lb. ground sausage

½ tsp. salt

2 tsp. freshly ground black pepper

2 ready-to-bake puff pastry sheets

1 egg, beaten, to glaze

Makes 20

Pre-heat the oven to 400°F, and lightly oil a large sheet baking pan. Mix the garlic, parsley, sage, and cayenne pepper, and stir in 3 tablespoons cold water. Place the sausage meat in a large bowl, add the garlic mixture, salt and plenty of freshly ground black pepper, and combine well, using your hands.

Unroll the pastry onto a lightly floured work surface and cut each one in half lengthwise. Divide the ground sausage into 4, and spread down the length of each pastry strip in a cylinder shape, leaving a ½-inch border. Brush the border with beaten egg. Tightly roll the pastry around the sausage and seal well. Using a sharp knife, cut each roll into 5 pieces, and transfer to a baking sheet, with the seal underneath. Brush each piece with beaten egg to glaze, and bake for about 30 minutes, or until the pastry is puffed, and crisp and golden, and the meat has cooked through. Cool on a wire rack. Store in an airtight container in the refrigerator until required, and serve cold or warm, with fresh tomato and red onion salsa (see page 25).

NOW TRY THIS

sausage and pepper rolls
Add 1 chopped, cooked red bell pepper to the sausage mix. Bake as before.

curried potato pasties
Omit the garlic, parsley, sage, cayenne pepper, and ground sausage. Fry 1 chopped onion, 2 teaspoons curry paste, and 1 teaspoon black mustard seeds, in a little oil until soft. Carefully stir in 10 ounces cooked cubed potatoes and 4 ounces cooked peas, juice of ½ lemon and 4 tablespoons chopped cilantro. Cool slightly, and use as above. Bake as before.

poppy seed breadsticks

These crunchy Italian breadsticks are delicious eaten as they are or served with a tangy dip. If you're feeling adventurous, try making a few different varieties to serve together.

1 ¼ cups/6 oz. white bread flour
1 tsp. dried yeast
½ tsp. salt
1 tbsp. olive oil
½ cup/4 fl. oz. warm water
2 tsp. poppy seeds
Makes about 24

Combine the flour, yeast, and salt in a large bowl and make a well in the center. Pour in the oil and water and mix until a soft dough forms.

Turn out the dough onto a lightly floured surface and knead it for 5–10 minutes, until it is smooth and elastic. Place the dough in a large, clean, oiled bowl, cover with oiled plastic wrap, and leave to rise in a warm place for about 1 hour or until doubled in size.

Preheat the oven to 400°F and lightly grease two baking sheets. Roll out the dough on a lightly floured surface into a rectangle that is 6 x 12 inches. Cut the dough into ½-inch-wide strips. Lightly roll the strips and arrange on the baking sheet, spacing them well apart.

Brush the grissini with water, sprinkle with poppy seeds, and bake for 10–12 minutes, until golden. Transfer to a wire rack to cool.

NOW TRY THIS

chunky breadstick twists
Cut the dough into ¾-inch-wide strips. Gently twist each strip and lay it on the baking sheet. Bake for about 15 minutes.

sesame seed breadsticks
Use sesame seeds in place of the poppy seeds.

parmesan breadsticks
Prepare the basic grissini recipe, using about 2 tablespoons of freshly grated Parmesan cheese in place of the poppy seeds.

fennel seed breadsticks
Use fennel seeds in place of the poppy seeds.

pea & mint tortilla

This tortilla is great to serve in bite-size pieces with drinks or with a simple salad as a more formal appetizer.

2 tbsp. olive oil

2 Spanish onions, halved and sliced thinly

1 ½ cups/8 oz. frozen peas, thawed

6 eggs

2 tsp. chopped fresh mint

salt and freshly ground black pepper

Serves 8

Heat the oil in a 9-inch nonstick skillet. Add the onion, sprinkle with salt, and fry gently for about 25 minutes, until tender. Season to taste, then stir in the peas.

Beat the eggs with the mint, and salt and pepper, then pour them over the onions and peas. Cook gently for about 10 minutes, pulling away the edges of the tortilla as it sets, to allow the uncooked egg to run underneath.

Meanwhile, preheat the broiler. When the tortilla is firm but still moist on top, brown the top under the broiler for about 5 minutes, until golden and set. Allow to cool for a few minutes.

Cover the pan with a plate and carefully invert both pan and plate. Remove the pan. Place another plate on top of the tortilla and invert both plates and tortilla to turn it right-side up. Serve warm or at room temperature, cut into wedges or bite-size pieces.

NOW TRY THIS

traditional tortilla
Use 1 ¾ cups/10 ounces sliced cooked potatoes in place of the peas, and 1 teaspoon fresh thyme leaves in place of the mint.

spicy sausage tortilla
Add ¼ cup/2 ounces thinly sliced chorizo with the onions.

sun-dried tomato tortilla
Add 4 sliced sun-dried tomatoes in oil with the peas.

fava bean tortilla
Use lightly cooked fava beans in place of the peas.

mini bacon & mushroom bites

These little bites are delightful with drinks as they are light and full of flavor.

¼ cup/2 oz. butter, plus extra for greasing

1 cup/5 oz. all-purpose flour

1 tsp. baking powder

1 tsp. salt

1 large egg

1 cup/8 fl. oz. whole milk

1 egg, beaten, for glaze

for the filling

4 tbsp. butter

4 slices smoked bacon, finely chopped

16 small mushrooms, finely chopped, plus extra for topping

1 large onion, finely chopped

salt and freshly ground black pepper

Makes 24

First make the filling. In a small skillet, melt the butter, and sauté the bacon, mushrooms and onion over low-medium heat, for 20–25 minutes, or until the juices have evaporated and the bacon is well cooked. Season well, with salt and freshly ground black pepper. Set aside to cool while you make the muffins.

Preheat the oven to 400°F, and grease 2 x 12-cup mini muffin pans with plenty of butter. In a small pan, over a gentle heat, melt the butter and set aside to cool slightly.

In a large bowl, whisk together the flour, baking powder, and salt. In another medium bowl, whisk the egg, milk, and melted butter. Make a well in the center of the flour mixture and quickly pour in the egg mixture and the filling. Stir gently until just combined, and do not over-mix. Spoon into the muffin cups, ¾ full, and brush the surface with beaten egg. Add half a small mushroom to the top of each one, and bake for about 20–22 minutes, until well risen and golden. Let cool in the pan for 5 minutes before turning out onto a wire tray to cool completely. Store in an airtight container until required, and serve warm if possible.

NOW TRY THIS

goat cheese & tomato bites
Omit the filling and the butter from the recipe. Instead, fold ¾ cup/4 ounces cubed goat cheese, ¾ cup/4 ounces chopped sundried tomatoes, and 4 teaspoons of fresh thyme into the mix, and bake as before.

cashew nut & cilantro bites
Omit the filling. Combine 4 teaspoons curry paste, ¾ cup/4 ounces toasted chopped cashew nuts, 4 teaspoons freshly chopped cilantro, and fold into the mixture. Bake as before.

dips

These dips are perfect with tortilla chips, as well as thinly sliced raw vegetables. Fresh-tasting tomato salsa, bursting with summer flavors, and creamy, richly flavored cheese dips are sure to be a hit with your friends and family.

tortilla chips

Serve these crunchy golden chips on their own or Mexican-style
with a spicy salsa or creamy guacamole.

2 soft flour tortillas
vegetable oil, for deep-frying
coarse sea salt, for sprinkling
Serves 4

Cut each tortilla into eight wedges. Pour oil into a deep frying pan until it is two-thirds full and heat to about 375°F, or until a cube of bread turns golden in about 1 minute.

Working in batches, add the tortilla wedges to the oil and fry for about 2 minutes, until golden. Remove from the oil using a slotted spoon and drain on paper towels. Sprinkle with salt before serving. Store in a plastic container until ready to eat.

NOW TRY THIS

smoky tortilla chips
Dust the tortilla chips with paprika just before serving.

tortilla chips with lime
Dust the tortilla chips with the finely grated zest of ½ lime just before serving.

curried tortilla chips
Dust the tortilla chips with curry powder just before serving.

fiery tortilla chips
Dust the tortilla chips with cayenne pepper just before serving.

fresh tomato & red onion salsa

Fresh and tangy, this peppery tomato salsa is simple to prepare and makes a great informal summery appetizer. For a Mexican feel, serve some tortilla chips or quesadilla wedges with it.

3 tomatoes, seeded and finely chopped

1 red onion, quartered and finely sliced

1 green chile pepper, seeded and finely chopped

3 good pinches of ground cumin

1 tsp. red wine vinegar

1 tbsp. olive oil

salt

2 tbsp. chopped fresh cilantro

Serves 4

Put the tomatoes, onion, chile pepper, cumin, vinegar, and oil in a bowl. Season with salt and toss to combine. Add the cilantro and toss again. Serve.

NOW TRY THIS

tomato & red onion salsa with basil
Replace the cilantro with a handful of basil.

tomato, bell pepper & red onion salsa
Preheat the oven to 450°F and roast 1 red bell pepper for about 30 minutes. Put in a bowl, cover with plastic wrap, and leave for 10 minutes. Peel, seed, and finely chop the pepper. Add to the salsa with the tomatoes.

tomato & scallion salsa
Add a bunch of finely sliced scallions in place of the red onion.

mild tomato & red onion salsa
Omit the green chile and add a good grinding of black pepper or a pinch of paprika instead.

spinach & artichoke dip

The richness of the wonderful combination of flavors of cheese and spinach, spiked with artichokes, will go beautifully with bread, chips, or toast.

2 x 12-oz. cans artichoke hearts in water, drained

½ cup/3 oz. chopped frozen spinach, thawed

1 cup/8 oz. full fat cream cheese, room temperature

½ cup/2 oz. grated Parmesan cheese

2 tbsp. freshly squeezed lemon juice

1 tsp. crushed red pepper flakes

¼ tsp. garlic powder

salt and freshly ground black pepper

¼ cup/1 oz. breadcrumbs

Serves 6

Preheat the oven to 350°F. Place the artichoke hearts in a food processor, and pulse until chopped. Transfer to a medium bowl, and combine with the spinach, cream cheese, Parmesan cheese, lemon juice, red pepper flakes, garlic powder, and salt and freshly ground black pepper.

Pour into a 9-inch baking dish, sprinkle with breadcrumbs, and bake for 30 minutes. Cool, cover, and refrigerate until required. To serve, cover with foil, and warm on the grill for 5 minutes.

NOW TRY THIS

artichoke & crab dip
Combine cream cheese, and 4 tablespoons each of mayonnaise and sour cream. Stir in 12 ounces each of artichoke hearts and crabmeat, ¼ cup/2 ounces each of Fontina and Pepper Jack cheese, 3 chopped scallions, 1 tablespoon Worcestershire sauce, salt and pepper. Spread in a skillet, sprinkle with more Fontina, and broil for 15 minutes.

roasted pepper & hummus dip
In a food processor, combine 2 cloves garlic, 14 ounces canned chickpeas, drained, ¼ cup tahini, and the juice of 2 lemons. Pulse until smooth. Add 1 roasted and sliced red bell pepper, ½ teaspoon dried basil, and pulse until peppers are finely chopped. Season well. Cover and chill until ready to serve.

minty cucumber & yogurt dip

This refreshing dip based on the classic Greek tzatziki makes a perfect light, informal appetizer. Serve it with pita bread or chips for scooping.

½ large cucumber
1 cup/8 oz. Greek yogurt
1 clove garlic, crushed
2 tbsp. chopped fresh mint
salt

Serves 4

Peel the cucumber, cut it in half lengthwise, and scrape out the seeds. Then grate the cucumber and place it in a sieve. Press out as much liquid as possible.

Place the cucumber in a bowl and mix in the yogurt, garlic, and mint. Season to taste with salt. Transfer to a serving bowl and chill until ready to serve.

NOW TRY THIS

garlicky cucumber & yogurt dip
Add an extra clove of crushed garlic.

spicy cucumber & yogurt dip
Add 1 seeded and finely chopped green chile.

cucumber, scallion & yogurt dip
Add 3 finely sliced scallions.

herb, cucumber & mint dip
Add 1 tablespoon snipped fresh chives and 1 tablespoon chopped fresh cilantro with the mint.

zucchini & caper dip

This light and tangy dip makes a healthy choice if you want a smooth, creamy dip without the calories. Serve it hot or cold with crackers or pita toasts.

3 zucchini, sliced
½ clove garlic, crushed
2 tsp. capers, rinsed
good pinch of dried chili flakes
2 tbsp. olive oil
salt
juice of ¼ lemon, to taste
Serves 4

Steam the zucchini for about 5 minutes, until tender.

Put the zucchini in a food processor and add the garlic, capers, chili flakes, and olive oil. Process to a smooth purée. Add salt and lemon juice to taste.

Transfer the dip to a bowl and serve hot or at room temperature.

NOW TRY THIS

lemon, zucchini & caper dip
Add ½ teaspoon grated lemon zest with the lemon juice.

creamy zucchini & caper dip
Omit the chili flakes and add 3 tablespoons crème fraîche with the lemon juice.

zucchini, caper & dill weed dip
Add 1 tablespoon chopped fresh dill weed and 2 tablespoons crème fraîche with the lemon juice.

minted zucchini & caper dip
Add 1 teaspoon chopped fresh mint to the food processor. Sprinkle with extra chopped fresh mint before serving.

subs &
sliders

No tailgating party is complete without hot dogs, subs, and sliders, which are tasty mini hamburger sandwiches!

biscuits with pepper, tomato & goat cheese

These yeasted biscuits can be stuffed with a variety of wonderful fillings.

4 tsp. sugar

1 ½ tsp. active dry yeast

2 ¼ cups/12 oz. all-purpose flour

3 tsp. baking powder

1 ½ tsp. salt

¼ tsp baking soda

1 tbsp. sugar

⅓ cup, plus 1 tbsp./3 oz. shortening

1 cup/8 fl. oz. buttermilk

for the filling

½ cup/4 oz. mayonnaise

3 tbsp. traditional basil pesto

11 oz. goat cheese, thinly sliced

1 x 11-oz. jar roasted peppers

2–3 large tomatoes, thinly sliced

Makes 18

Pour 4 tablespoons of warm water into a large bowl, stir in 1 teaspoon of the sugar, sprinkle with the yeast, and set aside for 10–15 minutes until frothy. In a separate bowl, whisk together the flour, baking powder, salt, baking soda, and remaining sugar. Cut in the shortening, using your fingers, until the mixture resembles breadcrumbs. Make a well in the center, and add the buttermilk and yeast mixture, stirring with a fork until just combined.

Turn the dough out onto a lightly floured work surface and knead a few times. Roll out to ½-inch thickness, and using a 2 ½-inch cutter, cut out about 18 biscuits, re-rolling as necessary. Place on the baking sheets, cover, and set aside to rise in a warm place for about an hour. Preheat the oven to 425°F. Bake the biscuits for 10–12 minutes, until golden. Cool on wire racks.

In a small bowl, mix the mayonnaise with the pesto. To serve, split the biscuits in half, spread each bottom half with pesto mayonnaise, add 2 slices goat cheese, red pepper, and sliced tomato, and top with the other half of the biscuit.

NOW TRY THIS

ham & mustard
Mix ½ cup/4 ounces softened butter with 2 tablespoons Dijon mustard and use to generously spread the bottom half of each biscuit. Fill all the biscuits with sliced ham.

bacon, lettuce & tomato
Spread the biscuits with mayonnaise, and fill with crispy bacon, lettuce leaves, and thin slices of tomato.

smoked salmon, red onion & lettuce
Spread the biscuits with softened butter, and fill with sliced smoked salmon, very thin slices of red onion and lettuce leaves.

garlic bread

Wrapping a whole loaf of bread in foil is the classic way to cook garlic bread. You can also grill unbuttered bread for about 2 minutes, brush with the butter mixture, and then grill again for 1 to 2 minutes.

1 loaf Italian or French bread
½ cup/4 oz. butter, softened
2 large cloves garlic, crushed
1 tsp. dried parsley flakes
¼ tsp. crumbled dried oregano
¼ tsp. dried dill weed
grated Parmesan cheese, to taste
dried parsley flakes, for sprinkling

Serves 4

Cut the bread into 1-inch slices but do not cut all the way through.

Blend the butter, garlic, parsley, oregano, and dill weed. Spread this mixture on both sides of the bread slices. Put the loaf back together on a large piece of aluminum foil and shape the foil around the loaf of bread. Twist the ends of the foil to seal, but leave the top open.

Sprinkle the top liberally with cheese and additional parsley flakes. Place on the grill away from direct heat and cook for 30 minutes to 1 hour, until lightly toasted. The timing will depend on the temperature.

NOW TRY THIS

parsley-garlic bread
Replace the oregano and dill weed with 2 additional tablespoons parsley flakes.

provolone-garlic bread
Replace the parsley, oregano, dill weed, and Parmesan with 1 teaspoon Worcestershire sauce and 1 ½ cups/6 ounces grated provolone cheese.

most delicious garlic-cheese bread
Mix 4 tablespoons olive oil, 4 large pressed cloves garlic, ⅔ cup/5 ounces mayonnaise, and 1 cup/4 ounces grated Parmesan. Prepare and cook as above, omitting the Parmesan cheese and dried parsley sprinkled on top.

hot beef sandwiches

This is a hearty meal sandwich.

8 oz. beef round tip steak, about ¼ in. thick

1 tbsp. olive oil

1 clove garlic, minced

1 ½ tbsp. soy sauce

black pepper

½ medium red onion, sliced

2 oz. mushrooms, sliced

2 tbsp. red wine or water

1 tsp. Dijon mustard

mini baguettes

Serves 4

Cut the steak in half, then into 1-inch strips, slicing across the grain. Heat the olive oil in a skillet, then add the beef and garlic and stir-fry until the meat is browned, about 2 minutes. Put in a dish with the soy sauce and black pepper, toss, and keep warm.

Using the same skillet, stir-fry the onion until soft, about 4 minutes, then add the mushrooms and cook until tender, about 3 minutes. Add the wine or water, mustard, and beef mixture. Bring to a boil, heat through, then divide the mixture among the rolls.

NOW TRY THIS

hot beef gyros
Omit mushrooms, red wine, mustard, and rolls. Stuff the hot beef into pita bread and top with Minty Cucumber & Yogurt Dip (see page 28).

wasabi beef sandwiches
Omit mushrooms, red wine, and mustard. Add 2 tablespoons grainy mustard, 2 teaspoons honey, and ½ teaspoon wasabi paste.

beef & blue sandwiches
Omit mushrooms, red wine, and mustard. In a small bowl, crumble ¼ cup/2 ounces Stilton or Roquefort cheese and mix with ¼ cup/2 ounces sour cream and 2 tablespoons mayonnaise. Spread over the base of the rolls before adding the beef. Add slices of tomato, if desired.

bacon wrapped hot dogs

Hot dogs are a must for any tailgating event, but make them a little special by wrapping them in bacon and serving with a delicious blend of tomato, red onion, and jalapeño.

3 tomatoes, chopped
½ red onion, chopped
1 jalapeño pepper, finely chopped
8 slices bacon
8 hot dog sausages
8 hot dog buns
5 tbsp. mayonnaise
tomato ketchup and yellow mustard, to serve

Serves 8

In a small bowl, mix together the tomato, onion, and pepper, and set aside.

Wrap one slice of bacon tightly around each hot dog sausage. Grill 8–10 minutes, turning each one occasionally, until the bacon is cooked and crispy on the edges, and the hot dogs are heated through.

Brush the bun halves with mayonnaise, and grill until lightly toasted. Fill each bun with a bacon wrapped hot dog sausage, and top with the onion mixture, ketchup, and mustard.

NOW TRY THIS

hot dogs with barbecue sauce
Make a barbeque sauce. Combine 1 cup/8 fluid ounces tomato ketchup, ¾ cup/5 ounces brown sugar, ½ cup/8 fluid ounces dry sherry, 2 tablespoons finely chopped fresh ginger, 3 crushed garlic cloves, 1 tablespoon Dijon mustard, ½ cup/4 fluid ounces soy sauce, and 3 tablespoons Worcestershire sauce. Serve with the hot dogs.

hot dogs with caramelized onions
Heat 2 tablespoons oil in a skillet, add 3 large onions, and ¼ teaspoon salt, and cook very slowly for 15-20 minutes, stirring occasionally. Add 2 tablespoons brown sugar and 2 tablespoons balsamic vinegar. Cook over low heat for a further 5-10 minutes, stirring occasionally, until sticky and caramelized. Cover and chill until required.

teriyaki chicken sub

The rich teriyaki sauce contrasts beautifully with the simple flavor of the chicken.

¾ cup/6 fl. oz. soy sauce

¼ cup/2 oz. brown sugar

3 tbsp. honey

2 tbsp. white wine vinegar

⅔ cup/5 fl. oz. orange juice

1 tsp. garlic paste

2 tsp. fresh ginger root, finely chopped

4 tbsp. cold chicken stock

3 tsp. cornstarch

2 tbsp. sesame oil

1 ¼ lbs chicken fillet, cut into strips

1 red bell pepper, sliced

1 small onion, finely sliced

6 submarine rolls

1 ¼ cups/6 oz. Swiss cheese, finely grated

Serves 6

In a medium bowl, mix together the soy sauce, brown sugar, honey, vinegar, orange juice, garlic, and ginger root. In a separate bowl, whisk the cornstarch and chicken stock together, and pour into the teriyaki sauce, mixing to combine.

Heat 1 tablespoon of the sesame oil in a large skillet, and when it is hot, but not smoking, add the chicken strips. Fry for 4–5 minutes each side, until the chicken has browned and is cooked through. Remove from the skillet, and set aside. Heat the remaining sesame oil in the skillet, add the red pepper and onion, and sauté for about 5 minutes, until beginning to brown. Remove from the pan. Preheat the oven to 400°F. Return the teriyaki sauce to the skillet and bring to a boil. Reduce the heat, add the chicken, peppers, onions. Simmer for 5 minutes, stirring frequently, until the sauce has thickened. Remove from the heat and leave to cool.

Cut each sub almost in half, and place cut side down on the grill until toasted. Put each roll on a square of foil, stuff with the teriyaki chicken, and top with cheese. Roll up tightly in the foil, put on a baking sheet and return to the grill for 3–4 minutes, until hot.

NOW TRY THIS

roasted vegetable marinara sub
Grill the subs as above. Fill with roasted vegetables (see page 66), add 2 tablespoons tomato sauce to each sub, wrap in foil, and heat as before.

ham, tomato & beet sub
Grill the subs as above. Spread each sub with mayonnaise, and fill with ham, sliced tomato and sliced pickled beet. Serve immediately.

bacon & cheddar sliders

These baby hamburgers have that wonderful combination of bacon and cheddar cheese, and are an ideal size for little hands.

12 oz. ground sirloin

3 shallots, finely chopped

1 tsp. Dijon mustard

cooking spray

½ cup/3 oz. grated Cheddar cheese

8 whole wheat slider buns

3 tbsp. mayonnaise

4 small dill pickles, cut lengthwise into 4

4 small lettuce leaves, cut into 2

1 ripe tomato, cut into 8 slices

3 slices bacon, cooked until crispy, and cut into 1-in. pieces

salt and freshly ground black pepper

Serves 6

Gently mix the sirloin with the shallots, Dijon mustard, salt and plenty of freshly ground black pepper. Divide into 8 portions and form into patties.

Spray the grill with cooking spray, and place the patties on the grill. Cook for 2–3 minutes each side, topping each one with 1 tablespoon cheese during the last minute of cooking.

Spray the cut sides of the slider buns and grill until nicely toasted. Spread the bottom half of each bun with mayonnaise, add a patty, two slices of dill pickle, ½ lettuce leaf, 1 slice of tomato, and bacon pieces. Season with freshly ground black pepper, and top with the other half of the slider buns. Serve immediately.

NOW TRY THIS

california sliders with guacamole
Omit the mayonnaise, dill pickles, lettuce, and bacon. Mash 2 avocados with the juice of ½ lime. Stir in 1 tablespoon freshly chopped cilantro, 1 minced clove garlic, ½ teaspoon salt, and ¼ teaspoon cayenne pepper. Spread the slider buns with butter and grill as before. Assemble the sliders with the guacamole on top of the patties and cheese.

chipotle chicken sliders
Omit the dill pickles and bacon. Assemble the sliders using Chipotle Popcorn Chicken (see page 10), and the rest of the ingredients.

dixie burgers with chowchow dressing
Omit the dill pickles and bacon, and substitute chowchow dressing, made by mixing ½ cup chowchow with 3 tablespoons mayonnaise.

barbecues & grills

In this chapter you will find all the classic burger, ribs, and pulled-pork recipes that are traditionally served at tailgating events, as well as innovative ideas to excite your more adventurous guests.

herbed beer can chicken

Steaming a chicken over a half-filled beer can infuse it with a delicious flavor.

1 whole chicken (4–5 lbs)
12-oz. can beer
(room temperature)
1 clove garlic, minced
1 sprig fresh rosemary, chopped
1 tsp. dried thyme

for the rub
2 tbsp. sugar
2 tbsp. garlic salt
1 tbsp. paprika
1 tsp. dried thyme
1 tsp. ground black pepper
1 tsp. grated lemon zest
¼ tsp. dried rosemary

Serves 6

Combine all the rub ingredients in a small mixing bowl and set aside. Remove the giblets and neck from the chicken. Sprinkle all over with rub, including inside the cavity. Open the can of beer and discard half of it. Place the minced garlic, rosemary, and thyme in the can and pierce two more holes into the top of beer can. Place the chicken over the can by pushing the can into the cavity of the chicken.

Preheat the grill. Place the bird on the grill, balanced by the beer can. Grill over indirect medium heat for 2 ½–3 ½ hours or until the internal temperature of the thigh is 165–180°F.

Wearing barbecue mitts, carefully remove the chicken and the can from the grill, being careful not to spill the beer—it will be hot. Let the chicken rest for about 10 minutes before lifting it from the can. Discard the beer. Cut the chicken into serving pieces. Serve warm.

NOW TRY THIS

root beer can chicken
Use the following rub mixture: 1 tablespoon paprika, 1 teaspoon dry mustard, 1 teaspoon each of onion powder and sea salt, and ½ teaspoon each of garlic powder, ground coriander, ground cumin, and freshly ground black pepper. Replace the beer can with a 12-ounce can of root beer.

sweet california beer can chicken
Use the following rub mixture: 2 tablespoons light brown sugar, 1 tablespoon each of sugar and smoked paprika, 1 ½ teaspoons garlic powder, sea salt to taste, 1 teaspoon pepper, ½ teaspoon dry mustard, and ¼ teaspoon each of cayenne pepper, dried ground sage, and poultry seasoning. Replace the beer with a can half-filled with white wine.

teriyaki pork burger

In Japanese, *teri* means "sunshine" and *yaki* means "roast" or "grilled," so what could be more suitable for barbecuing?

1 ½ lbs ground pork
4 tbsp. fine dry breadcrumbs
¼ tsp. freshly ground black pepper
2 tbsp. finely chopped onion
3 scallions, thinly sliced
1 large clove garlic, crushed
3 tbsp. soy sauce
2 tbsp. orange juice concentrate
2 tsp. ground ginger
2 tbsp. light brown sugar

Makes 4–6

Combine all the ingredients together in a bowl. Use your hands to form the mixture into 4 to 6 patties.

Grill over medium heat for 5–10 minutes on each side or until no pink remains. Always cook ground pork to well done or 165˚F. Serve on hamburger buns with your favorite condiments and garnish.

For a new taste sensation, serve on a hamburger or kaiser bun with a layer of oranges, sliced kiwi fruit, and sliced strawberries on top.

NOW TRY THIS

herbed pork burgers
Replace the soy sauce, orange juice, ginger, and sugar with 5 tablespoons brandy, 1 tablespoon celery salt, 2 teaspoons each of dried sage and dried rosemary, 1 teaspoon freshly ground pepper, ½ teaspoon each of dried thyme and crumbled dried summer savory, ¼ teaspoon freshly grated nutmeg, and 1 teaspoon oil. Proceed as above.

brat burgers
Replace the soy sauce, orange juice, ginger, and sugar with 2 teaspoons each of salt, sugar, dry mustard, paprika, ground coriander, dried sage, and freshly ground pepper; and ¼ teaspoon each of dried rosemary, grated nutmeg, and cayenne pepper. Proceed as above.

north carolina style pulled pork

This delicious pork dish can be fully or partly prepared in advance.

1 tbsp. smoked paprika

1 tbsp. brown sugar

1 tsp. freshly ground black pepper

½ tsp. each of cayenne pepper, celery salt, garlic salt, dry mustard powder, onion powder

¼ tsp. salt

6–8 lbs pork shoulder

for the piquant vinegar basting sauce

1 ½ cups/12 fl. oz. cider vinegar

1 cup/8 fl. oz. water

½ cup/4 oz. tomato ketchup

¼ cup/2 oz. brown sugar

2 tbsp. soy sauce

2 tsp. crushed red pepper flakes

salt and freshly ground black pepper

Serves 10

In a small bowl, mix together the smoked paprika, brown sugar, black pepper, cayenne pepper, celery, and garlic salt, dry mustard, onion powder, and salt. Rub this mixture into the pork on all sides, wrap in plastic wrap, and refrigerate for 8 hours, or overnight.

In a small pan, combine all the ingredients for the sauce. Bring to a boil, and remove from heat. Save about 1 ½ cups/12 fluid ounces of the liquid for serving; use the rest for basting.

Preheat the oven to 250°F. Remove the plastic wrap, place the pork in a foil-lined roasting pan, and sprinkle with salt and pepper. Pour in the basting liquid, cover tightly with foil, and roast for 7 hours. Remove from the oven and let cool for 15 minutes. Shred the meat into bite-size pieces using two forks. Pour some of the basting sauce over the pork, and serve immediately.

Alternatively, cook uncovered on a very low grill, on indirect heat over a drip pan. Cover grill, and cook the pork until it shreds easily, about 7 hours. Check hourly, adding extra coals if necessary to maintain heat and smoke.

NOW TRY THIS

pulled pork with barbecue sauce
Make only half the marinade, and instead of serving with the marinade, serve with barbecue sauce (see page 36).

pulled pork & coleslaw sandwiches
Use the barbecue sauce method above. Divide the pulled pork between as many burger buns as required, and top with coleslaw.

cajun grilled chicken skewers

Soak wooden skewers in water so that they do not burn on the grill, and you will be rewarded with succulent chicken enhanced with charred vegetables.

3 cloves garlic, finely chopped

½-in. piece fresh ginger root, finely chopped

zest and juice of 1 orange

2 tbsp. honey

1 tbsp. soy sauce

2 tbsp. vegetable oil

4 chicken breasts, cut into 1-in. pieces

20 button mushrooms

20 grape tomatoes

2 red bell peppers, each one cut into 10 pieces

salt and freshly ground black pepper

Makes 20 skewers

Place the garlic, ginger root, orange zest and juice, honey, soy sauce, and oil in a food processor, and pulse until smooth.

Place the chicken in a medium bowl, pour over the sauce, cover, and leave to marinate for anything from an hour to overnight. Add the mushrooms for the last 30 minutes.

Thread the chicken, mushrooms, tomatoes and peppers onto 20 wooden skewers, and season with salt and freshly ground black pepper. Cook on the grill for 7–8 minutes each side, or until the chicken is golden brown and cooked through, turning the skewers occasionally, and basting with the sauce. Serve immediately.

NOW TRY THIS

korean beef kebabs
Make a marinade with 6 tablespoons soy sauce, 1 ½ tablespoons each of sesame seeds and sesame oil, 2 minced cloves garlic, 2 teaspoons sugar, salt and freshly ground black pepper. Cut 1 pound sirloin steak into 1-inch pieces and marinate for 1–8 hours. Thread the beef on the skewers with the vegetables, and cook as before.

vegetable souvlaki skewers
Cut 1 eggplant, 2 red onions, 2 yellow bell peppers, and 2 cups/10 ounces halloumi cheese into 1-inch chunks and thread onto the skewers with 10 button mushrooms, and 20 grape tomatoes. Drizzle with olive oil and freshly squeezed lemon juice, season well, and grill as above. Serve with warm pita bread.

barbecued beef rib racks

Grilling baby beef ribs is a traditional technique. The ingredients for this rub and sauce are often on hand, making the dish a reliable standby.

for the dry rub

2 tbsp. freshly ground black pepper

1 tbsp. garlic salt

1 tbsp. onion salt

1 tbsp. sweet paprika

1 tsp. cayenne pepper, or to taste

1 slab baby beef ribs

for the mopping sauce

4 tbsp. canola oil

juice of 1 large lemon

2 tbsp. ketchup

1 tsp. freshly ground black pepper

1 tsp. dry mustard

Serves 4

Combine the dry rub ingredients and blend well. Season the ribs on both sides with the rub. Combine all the ingredients for the mopping sauce in a small saucepan. Heat for 10 minutes over medium or low heat.

Cook the ribs using the indirect heat method at between 230°F and 250°F for about 4–6 hours, depending on the size of the ribs. Turn the ribs after cooking 2 hours and brush with a light coat of the mopping sauce. Cook until the ribs are tender, mopping them occasionally. The ribs are done when they are pierced easily with a knife.

NOW TRY THIS

big bill's beef ribs
Replace the rub with one made by mixing 4 tablespoons salt, 2 tablespoons each of paprika and coarse ground black pepper, 1 ½ teaspoons each of garlic powder, onion powder, and cayenne pepper, and ½ teaspoon each of ground coriander and turmeric.

tender smoked beef ribs
Replace the rub with one made by combining 3 tablespoons sugar, 2 tablespoons each of onion powder, garlic powder, salt, 1 tablespoon each of black pepper and paprika, 2 teaspoons each of seasoned salt and dried oregano, and ½ teaspoon each of dried sage, grated nutmeg, and cayenne.

spicy lamb koftas

These lightly spiced lamb skewers make a tasty start to any meal. Serve with a tomato salsa and, if you like, a chopped vegetable salad as well.

8 oz. lean ground lamb
2 large scallions, finely chopped
1 clove garlic, crushed
1 tsp. ground cumin
1 tsp. ground coriander
¼ tsp. cayenne pepper
2 tsp. chopped fresh mint
salt and ground black pepper
fresh tomato & red onion salsa
(see page 25), to serve

Serves 4

Soak 8 wooden toothpicks in cold water for 15 minutes.

In a bowl, mix the lamb, scallions, garlic, cumin, coriander, cayenne, and mint until combined. Season well with salt and pepper. Use your hands to mix the ingredients thoroughly.

Divide the mixture into 8 portions, and shape them into small egg-shaped balls. Thread each ball onto a toothpick and press it out to form a sausage shape. Chill for about 30 minutes.

Preheat the broiler. Broil the skewers for 5–8 minutes, turning once or twice, until cooked through. Serve with tomato salsa.

NOW TRY THIS

lamb kofta wraps
Serve the koftas and salsa wrapped in quartered flour tortillas.

beef koftas
Use ground beef instead of lamb.

chicken or turkey koftas
Use ground chicken or turkey instead of lamb.

harissa-spiced lamb koftas
Use 1 to 2 teaspoons harissa in place of the cumin, coriander, and cayenne.

lemon lamb koftas
Add the grated zest of ½ lemon with the spices.

sticky sweet & spicy chicken wings

The Chinese-inspired sauce for these chicken wings is made with hoisin sauce sweetened with brown sugar and spiced up with a little horseradish.

3 lbs chicken wings

salt and freshly ground black pepper

canola oil, for deep-frying

for the sauce

1 cup/8 fl. oz. hoisin sauce

½ cup/4 fl. oz. cranberry juice

¼ cup/2 oz. brown sugar

2 cloves garlic, finely chopped

1 tbsp. prepared horseradish

4 scallions, finely chopped

salt and freshly ground black pepper

Serves 6

Place the chicken wings on a baking sheet, and season both sides with salt and freshly ground black pepper. Set aside for 1 hour.

In a small pan, mix together all the sauce ingredients. Bring to a boil, stirring continuously, reduce the heat to a simmer, and cook for about 20 minutes, until thickened, stirring frequently. Taste and adjust the seasoning.

In a large pan, over a medium-high heat, place enough canola oil to come half way up the sides, and using a thermometer, heat until it is 350°F. Deep-fry the wings in batches for about 6 minutes, turning them occasionally, or until golden brown, and cooked through. Drain on paper towels. Put half the wings in a large bowl, add half of the sauce and toss together until well coated. Repeat with the rest of the wings and sauce. Refrigerate until required. To reheat, spread the wings out on two large baking sheets and place on the grill for 10 minutes, until piping hot. Watch carefully to ensure they do not burn, turning them as necessary.

NOW TRY THIS

sticky, sweet & spicy chili wings
Add 1–2 teaspoons crushed red pepper flakes to the sauce. Alternatively, add a finely chopped red chile pepper, if you like it really hot.

sticky, sweet & spicy popcorn chicken
Make the Chipotle Popcorn Chicken (see page 10), and toss in the sauce as above.

tamari & honey thighs
Slash 8–10 chicken thighs, and place in a roasting pan. Mix 5 teaspoons vegetable oil, 4 tablespoons tamari soy sauce, 6 tablespoons rice wine, 10 tablespoons chopped stem ginger in syrup, 6 crushed cloves garlic, and 3–4 chopped red chiles. Pour over the chicken and bake at 350°F for 40–45 minutes. Drizzle with honey and broil for 3 minutes.

doug's jamaican jerk chicken

The secret to keeping any barbecued chicken moist is to use spray oil.

4 x jalapeño peppers, seeded and chopped

2 cloves garlic, finely chopped

2 scallions, chopped

1 tbsp. fresh thyme leaves

1 tbsp. ground allspice

1 tsp. Tobasco chipotle sauce

¾ tsp. ground cinnamon

1 tsp. freshly ground black pepper

2 tbsp. honey

1 tbsp. extra-virgin olive oil

2 tbsp. white wine vinegar

2 tbsp. soy sauce

1 tbsp. dark rum

zest and juice of 1 orange and 1 lime

1 ½ lbs chicken pieces, skin on

cooking spray

Serves 6

In a large bowl, mix all of the ingredients (except the chicken and cooking spray) for the marinade together and then transfer to a food processor. Pulse the ingreidents until they are fully combined.

Pour the marinade back into the large bowl and then add the chicken pieces, turning them around to coat them all over. Cover and refrigerate for anything from an hour to overnight.

Grill the chicken for about 15 minutes, or until cooked through. Turn it over frequently, and spray it each time with cooking spray to keep it moist. Serve immediately.

NOW TRY THIS

cajun chicken
Substitute Cajun seasoning, made by combining 2 tablespoons each of salt, cayenne pepper, paprika, garlic granules, ground black pepper, 1 tablespoon each of onion granules, oregano, and thyme. Cook and serve as before.

grilled chicken with fajita spices
Combine 2 teaspoons chili powder with 1 teaspoon each of salt, smoked paprika, sugar, and chicken bouillon powder, ½ teaspoon of onion powder, and ¼ teaspoon each of garlic powder, cayenne pepper, ground cumin, and ground coriander. Mix with the zest and juice of 2 limes, and marinade and cook the chicken as before.

salads & sides

From classic potato salad to an exotic quinoa and avocado salad, there is plenty to choose from in this chapter to accompany your grilled or barbecue fare.

barbecued corn on the cob

Here's the classic barbecue vegetable.

8 ears of corn with husks

3 tbsp. butter

1 tsp. chili powder

1 tsp. onion salt

freshly ground black pepper to taste

Serves 8

Pull the husks carefully from the corn so that each husk remains attached to the bottom of the ear. Remove any silk from the corn.

Melt the butter in a small saucepan, add the seasonings, and stir. Brush this butter mixture onto each ear of corn. Pull the corn husk up to cover the corn and wrap each piece in a sheet of heavy-duty aluminum foil.

Grill the corn directly over a medium-hot grill. Cook for 30–40 minutes, turning every few minutes. Carefully remove the foil and husk before serving.

NOW TRY THIS

corn on the cob with spicy lime butter
Make a flavored butter to serve with the corn: blend together 8 tablespoons unsalted butter, softened, grated zest of 1 lime, 1 canned chipotle chile, and salt to taste. Chill. Grill corn as above, serving a disc of the butter on top of each grilled ear so that it melts into the corn.

cajun-grilled corn on the cob
Roll grilled corn in a rub made from 1 teaspoon each of dried oregano and paprika, ¾ teaspoon each of garlic and onion powder, ½ teaspoon salt, ¼ teaspoon dried thyme and black pepper, and ¼ teaspoon cayenne.

quinoa & avocado salad

This appetizing salad will tempt even the most fussy family member.

1 cup/8 oz. quinoa

1 x 11-oz. can mandarin oranges

1 yellow bell pepper, seeded and diced

¼ cup/2 oz. dried cherries

4 scallions, finely sliced

1 avocado, peeled, pitted, and diced

¼ cup/2 oz. chopped pecans

3 tbsp. freshly chopped parsley

for the orange dressing

⅓ cup/3 fl. oz. extra-virgin olive oil

3 tbsp. white wine vinegar

2 tsp. Dijon mustard

2 tsp. lime juice

salt and freshly ground black pepper

Serves 4

In a large saucepan, bring 2 cups/16 fluid ounces water to a boil. Add the quinoa and simmer gently for 10–12 minutes, until all the water has been absorbed. Remove from the heat, fluff with a fork, cover, and set aside for 10 minutes. Transfer to a large bowl and let cool for 10 minutes.

Drain off 2 tablespoons of juice from the mandarin oranges for the dressing and whisk together with the rest of the dressing ingredients. Set aside.

Drain away the rest of the juice from the mandarin oranges and then add the oranges to the quinoa. Stir in the yellow bell pepper, dried cherries, and scallions. Cover and chill until required. Just before serving, add the avocado, chopped pecans, and parsley. Serve with the orange dressing.

NOW TRY THIS

quinoa & avocado salad with cranberries
Replace the cherries with dried cranberries.

quinoa & apple with honey dressing
Omit the avocado and mandarin oranges in the salad, and substitute 1 peeled, cored, and diced apple. Replace the orange juice in the dressing with 1 tablespoon honey.

brown rice & celery salad
Replace the quinoa with 2 ¾ cups/18 ounces cooked brown rice. Replace the orange dressing with an Asian dressing; whisk together 4 tablespoons soy sauce, 2 tablespoons Dijon mustard, ½ teaspoon sesame oil, ½ teaspoon minced ginger root, and 2 tablespoons water.

mixed tomato salad

Tomatoes love sugar, so the sweetness of the pomegranate in the dressing brings out their flavor beautifully. Use an assortment of tomato colors.

1 ½ lbs small tomatoes (in assorted colors, if possible)

¼ cup/2 oz. crumbled feta cheese

3 tbsp. freshly chopped cilantro, plus extra to serve

¼ cup/1 ½ oz. pomegranate seeds

for the dressing

1 ½ cups/12 fl. oz. pomegranate juice

2 tsp. lemon juice

2 tbsp. sugar

2 tbsp. extra-virgin olive oil

2 shallots, finely chopped

Serves 4

To make the dressing, simmer together the pomegranate juice, lemon juice, and sugar in a medium saucepan, over medium heat, until the liquid is thick and syrupy and has reduced to about 4 tablespoons. Set aside to cool. When cool, whisk together with the olive oil and shallots.

Just before serving, mix together the tomatoes, feta cheese, and cilantro in a serving bowl. Fold in the dressing. Sprinkle a little extra cilantro and the pomegranate seeds over the top. Serve immediately.

NOW TRY THIS

mixed tomato salad with chile salsa
Omit the dressing and pomegranate seeds. Make a chile salsa by mixing 1 small finely chopped red onion, 1 minced garlic clove, 1 ounce freshly chopped cilantro, 1 teaspoon extra-virgin olive oil, 1 teaspoon lime juice, 1 finely chopped red chile, and salt and pepper. Serve over the tomato salad.

mixed tomato & basil salad
Omit the dressing and pomegranate seeds and replace the cilantro with basil. Replace the dressing with a vinaigrette. Mix together 3 tablespoons extra-virgin olive oil, 1 tablespoon red wine vinegar, 1 finely chopped small shallot, and salt and freshly ground black pepper.

classic potato salad

Chopped potatoes, well seasoned with fresh parsley is the perfect salad for a picnic or tailgating party.

2 lbs small firm potatoes

⅓ cup/3 ½ fl. oz. good-quality mayonnaise

3 tbsp. extra-virgin olive oil

1 tbsp. white wine vinegar

3 tbsp. freshly chopped parsley

4 scallions, finely chopped

4 slices bacon, cooked until crispy, and crumbled

salt and freshly ground black pepper

Serves 6–8

In a large pan, bring the potatoes to a boil, and gently simmer for 20 minutes, until just cooked. Drain and set aside to cool.

Cut the potatoes into 1-inch cubes, and transfer to a large serving bowl. Season well, with salt and plenty of freshly ground black pepper.

In a medium bowl, combine the mayonnaise, olive oil, and vinegar, and mix gently into the potatoes with the parsley. Store in an airtight container in the refrigerator until required. Serve garnished with the scallions and bacon.

NOW TRY THIS

classic coleslaw
Finely slice a medium white cabbage, and a small onion. Grate 3 large carrots, and mix in a large bowl. Add 2 cups/16 fluid ounces mayonnaise and stir until blended. Season.

potato salad with capers & gherkins
Add ½ cup/4 ounces each of capers and finely sliced baby pickled gherkins.

grilled potato salad
Replace one-third of the potatoes with sweet potatoes, cutting them all into large chunks. Boil for 15 minutes. Toss the potatoes with ¼ cup/2 fluid ounces mayonnaise, 1 tablespoon Dijon mustard, 2 teaspoons each of garlic and onion powder, and place them on the grill for 1–2 minutes. Serve with the parsley and garnish as above.

roasted vegetable & orzo salad

Orzo is a small rice-shaped pasta that works very well in a cold salad.

1 small eggplant, cut into 1-in. dice

1 red bell pepper, cut into 1-in. dice

1 green bell pepper, cut into 1-in. dice

1 small red onion, cut into 1-in. dice

1 clove garlic clove, finely chopped

6 tbsp. extra-virgin olive oil, plus extra for greasing

8 grape tomatoes, halved

1 ¼ cups/8 oz. orzo

¼ cup/1 oz. pine nuts

2 tbsp. freshly squeezed lemon juice

1 cup/6 oz. feta cheese, crumbled

3 tbsp. freshly torn basil leaves

salt and freshly ground black pepper

Serves 6

Preheat the oven to 375°F, and lightly grease a large roasting pan with a little olive oil.

In a large bowl, toss together the eggplant, red and green bell peppers, onion, and garlic with 4 tablespoons of the olive oil, salt and freshly ground black pepper until the vegetables are well coated with the oil. Spread out on the roasting pan and roast for 30 minutes, until browned. Turn half way through cooking to roast both sides, and add the tomatoes and pine nuts to the roasting pan for the last 5 minutes cooking time.

In a large pan, cook the orzo for 7–9 minutes, until tender. Drain and transfer to a large serving bowl. Remove the vegetables from the oven and transfer to the serving bowl with any juices. When the pasta salad has cooled, stir in the remaining olive oil, lemon juice, feta cheese, basil leaves, salt and plenty of freshly ground black pepper. Store in an airtight container in the refrigerator until required.

NOW TRY THIS

with zucchini & goat cheese
Add 2 sliced zucchini to the vegetables, and roast as above. Replace the feta with goat cheese.

with corn & pasta penne
Replace the orzo with pasta penne, cooked as directed on the packet. Add 1 can (10 ounces) corn kernels, drained, to the salad.

roasted vegetable & rice salad
Omit the orzo. Boil 8 ounces basmati rice for 10 minutes, drain, and cool. Mix with the roasted vegetables, and serve as above.

grilled vegetable platter

The colors of the vegetables piled high on this platter look really spectacular.

1 lb. thick asparagus spears

2 zucchini

1 bunch carrots (about 8 oz.), peeled

1 red bell pepper

1 yellow bell pepper

1 large red onion, peeled

2 tbsp. vegetable oil

1 tbsp. fresh thyme

½ cup/4 fl. oz. balsamic vinegar

4 tbsp. maple syrup

salt and freshly ground black pepper

Serves 6

Trim the woody ends of the asparagus spears. Cut the zucchini and carrots lengthwise into thirds. Seed and core the red and yellow peppers; cut each into eighths. Set the onion on its root end and cut it into 8 wedges, leaving the end intact. Place the vegetables in a bowl. Toss the vegetables with the oil, thyme, salt, and pepper.

Place the vegetables on a grill preheated to medium. Cook for 3 minutes. Remove the asparagus and keep warm. Rotate the remaining vegetables 90 degrees to make crosshatched grill marks. Continue cooking, rotating every 3 minutes, until tender-crisp. Remove from the heat.

Meanwhile, in a small saucepan, bring the vinegar and maple syrup to a boil; boil until thickened, about 2 minutes. Brush one-quarter of the glaze over vegetables; turn over and brush again. Transfer to a serving platter and brush with remaining glaze.

NOW TRY THIS

with basil aïoli
Replace the dressing with a basil aïoli made by whisking together 1 tablespoon torn basil leaves, 2 pressed large cloves garlic, 1 egg yolk, 2 teaspoons fresh lemon juice, and ½ cup/4 fluid ounces olive oil. Add the oil gradually in a thin stream, not all at once. Put aïoli in a bowl to serve with the vegetables.

with fresh basil vinaigrette
Replace the dressing with a vinaigrette made by whisking together 1 cup/8 fluid ounces extra-virgin olive oil, ¼ cup/2 fluid ounces fresh lemon juice, 1 tablespoon chopped fresh basil, 2 pressed cloves garlic, and 1 tablespoon Dijon mustard.

patatas bravas

Patatas bravas simply translates as "fierce" potatoes. They are sliced fried potatoes smothered in a rich tomato sauce with a hint of smoky spiciness.

1 lb. waxy potatoes (such as Yukon Gold), well scrubbed

2 cups/16 fl. oz. mild olive oil

for the tomato sauce

3 tbsp. olive oil

1 small onion, finely chopped

1 clove garlic, finely chopped

1 small dried red chile, finely chopped

½ tsp. smoked paprika

4 large ripe plum tomatoes, chopped

2 tsp. tomato paste

salt and freshly ground black pepper

fresh flat-leaf parsley, to garnish (optional)

Serves 6

Cut the potatoes into even-sized chunks. Add them to a large pan half-filled with the oil and heat gently over a low flame until small bubbles rise to the surface. Cook the potatoes like this—almost poaching them in the oil—for around 12–15 minutes, until they are just tender. Then, increase the heat and deep-fry the potato pieces until golden brown.

While the potatoes are cooking, prepare the sauce. Heat the oil in a small saucepan. Fry the onion, garlic, and chile in the hot oil for 3–4 minutes, until softened but not colored. Stir in the paprika and cook for a few seconds more. Add the tomatoes to the pan. Stir in the tomato paste and ½ cup/4 fluid ounces water. Cook over low heat for about 10 minutes until the tomatoes are well softened, stirring occasionally. Season to taste with salt and pepper. Lift the potatoes out of the oil with a slotted spoon and drain on paper towels. Put into a warmed dish, add the tomato sauce, and serve.

NOW TRY THIS

patatas bravas with piquillo peppers
Add 2 chopped piquillo peppers (jarred roasted red peppers) to the sauce at the end of cooking.

patatas bravas with chorizo
Add slices of fried chorizo on top of the dish.

patatas bravas with blood sausage
Add 1 Spanish blood sausage, chopped and fried, to the cooked potatoes just before covering with the sauce.

black bean & corn salsa salad

This bean salad is absolutely bursting with flavor; the cilantro, salt, and pepper are essential for the sun-kissed vegetables to shine.

2 x 10-oz. cans black beans, rinsed

2 x 10-oz. cans corn kernels, drained

½ red onion, cut into ¼-in. dice

1 red bell pepper, cut into ¼-in. dice

1 green bell pepper, cut into ¼-in. dice

½ cup/4 fl. oz. extra-virgin olive oil

2 tbsp./1 oz. freshly chopped cilantro

salt and freshly ground black pepper

Serves 8

In a large bowl, mix all the ingredients together and season to taste with salt and freshly ground black pepper. Refrigerate until required, and serve cold.

NOW TRY THIS

with walnuts, scallions & pomegranate
Add ¼ cup/2 ounces chopped walnuts, 4 chopped scallions, and 4 tablespoons pomegranate seeds to the salad.

pinto bean, corn, avocado & tomatoes
Replace the black beans with pinto beans. Add 1 chopped avocado and 2 chopped tomatoes to the salad and serve as above.

chickpeas, cucumber, parsley, & mint
Substitute chickpeas for the black beans, 1 finely chopped cucumber for the corn kernels, and 1 tablespoon each of chopped parsley and mint for the cilantro.

cakes & bakes

Desserts are always popular at picnics!
How about Carrot Cake Cookie Sandwiches (page 74) or
mini Chocolate and Peanut Butter Tartlets (page 79)—
these are just two of the delectable little sweet morsels
you can find in this chapter to tempt your guests.

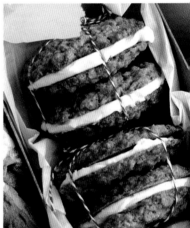

chocolate macadamia slice

This one is calories on a plate, but as an occasional treat, it is a winner.

½ cup/4 oz. butter

2 tbsp. unrefined dark brown sugar

4 tbsp. cocoa powder, sifted

3 tbsp. corn syrup

1 ¾ cups/8 oz. crushed graham crackers, peanut butter, or ginger cookies

½ cup/3 oz. macadamia nuts, roughly chopped

½ cup/3 oz. raisins

for the topping

1 ¾ cups/8 oz. semisweet chocolate, optional

Makes about 16

In a saucepan over medium low heat, melt the butter, sugar, cocoa and corn syrup until the sugar crystals disappear. Stir in the crushed cookies, nuts and raisins.

Line an 8-inch square cake pan with plastic wrap. Press the mixture into the pan and flatten with the back of a spoon. If using the topping, melt the chocolate over a double boiler, then smooth over the base. Mark into squares and set in the refrigerator. Cut when cold.

NOW TRY THIS

rocky road slice
Replace the nuts and raisins with ¼ cup/ 2 ounces mini marshmallows and ¼ cup/ 2 ounces each of white chocolate chips and peanuts.

chocolate–cherry almond slice
Replace the macadamia nuts and raisins with ¼ cup/2 ounces each of candied cherries chopped blanched almonds.

chocolate–apricot amaretti slice
Replace the cookies, macadamia nuts, and raisins with amaretti cookies and ¼ cup/2 ounces each apricots and chopped almonds.

chocolate, coconut & cranberry slice
Replace the macadamia nuts and raisins with ¼ cup/2 ounces each of flaked coconut and dried cranberries.

churros con chocolade

Churros are sausage-shaped doughnuts that are meant for plunging in the thick chocolate sauce served with them.

⅔ cup/5 ½ fl. oz. water

4 tbsp. vegetable oil

½ cup/2 oz. all-purpose flour

pinch salt

2 large eggs, room temperature

vegetable oil for deep-frying

⅓ cup/1 ¾ oz. superfine sugar

for the dipping sauce

¼ cup/2 oz. semisweet chocolate

⅔ cup/5 ½ fl. oz. heavy cream

Makes 12

Place the water in a saucepan with 4 tablespoons oil and bring to a boil. Mix the flour with the salt and gradually add it to the boiling water. Stir well with a wooden spoon over low heat until the mixture sticks together and leaves the sides of the pan. Remove from the heat and beat in the eggs.

In a heavy, large pan, heat the oil to 360°F. Spoon the churros mixture into a pastry bag fitted with a large star-shaped tip. Pipe two or three 4-inch lengths of dough at a time directly into the hot oil and cook for 2 minutes on each side, until crisp and golden. Drain the churros on paper towels and sprinkle with sugar. Repeat until all the churros mixture is used up.

To make the chocolate dip, gently warm the chocolate and cream together in a small saucepan. Stir until smooth, remove it from the heat, and transfer to a small bowl. Serve with a pile of the hot churros. Serve immediately.

NOW TRY THIS

cinnamon churros con chocolade
Add 1 teaspoon ground cinnamon to the granulated sugar.

churros con chocolade with chili
Add a pinch of chili powder to the chocolate sauce.

churros con dulce de leche
Replace the chocolate sauce with 3–4 tablespoons of dulce de leche.

churros con chocolade with orange
Add the zest of 1 orange to the chocolate sauce.

carrot cake cookie sandwiches

If you like carrot cake, you will love these little cookie sandwiches.

1 cup/8 oz. full fat cream cheese

½ cup/4 oz. butter

1 cup/4 oz. confectioners' sugar

for the cookies

2 cups/9 oz. all-purpose flour

1 tsp. each of baking powder, baking soda, ground cinnamon, pumpkin pie spice

½ tsp. ground nutmeg

¼ tsp. salt

1 cup/8 oz. butter, room temperature

1 cup/8 oz. each of granulated and brown sugar

2 eggs, room temperature

1 tsp. vanilla extract

2 cups/6 ½ oz. rolled oats

1 ½ cup/6 oz. finely grated carrots

4 tbsp. finely chopped walnuts

Makes 20 sandwiches

Mix the cream cheese with a wooden spoon to soften, and gradually add the butter, beating until smooth. Sift in the confectioners' sugar, and mix with a wooden spoon until slightly combined, then beat with an electric mixer until smooth. Chill in the refrigerator until firm, while you make the cookies.

Line 2 baking sheets with parchment. Sift the dry ingredients together. Beat the butter with the sugars until light and fluffy. Add the eggs one at a time, beating well between each one, add the vanilla, and beat until combined. Combine with the flour mixture, and mix in the oats, carrots, and walnuts. Chill in the refrigerator for 2 hours, until firm.

Preheat the oven to 350°F. Form the dough into 40 small balls on the baking sheets and bake for 12–15 minutes, until lightly browned and a little crisp on the edges. Cool on wire racks.

Once cooled completely, spread cream cheese frosting on half the cookies, and sandwich together with the remaining cookies. Store in an airtight container for 2 to 3 days in the refrigerator, and bring to room temperature before eating.

NOW TRY THIS

carrot cake & coffee cookie sandwiches
Replace the pumpkin pie spice with 2 teaspoons instant coffee powder and add 2 teaspoons instant coffee powder, mixed with 1 tablespoon hot water, to the filling.

tropical carrot cake cookie sandwiches
Replace ¼ cup/1 ounce of the rolled oats with flaked coconut.

chocolate & chestnut cookie sandwiches
Omit the filling. Make a chocolate filling by gently heating ¾ cup/4 ounces semisweet chocolate and ⅔ cup/5 fluid ounces whipping cream in a small pan until melted. Cool. Blend 2 ¼ cups/14 ounces canned chestnut purée with 1 tablespoon sugar, the chocolate cream, and 2 tablespoons brandy in a food processor until smooth, and fill as before.

blueberry crumble bars

You can make these sweet and fruity bars a day or two before you need them. Take them along to your tailagating party for a ready-prepared treat!

3 cups/13 ½ oz. all-purpose flour
1 cup/8 oz. sugar
1 tsp. baking powder
¼ tsp. salt
zest and juice of 1 lemon
1 cup/8 oz. cold butter
1 egg, lightly beaten
4 cups/1 lb. fresh blueberries
½ cup/3 ½ oz. sugar
4 tsp. cornstarch
Makes about 16

Preheat the oven to 375°F, and grease a 9 x 13-inch shallow baking pan.

In a large bowl, whisk together the flour, sugar, and baking powder. Add the salt and lemon zest. Cut the cold butter into small pieces, add to the flour mixture and using either your fingers or a pastry cutter, mix until the mixture resembles fine breadcrumbs. Stir in the egg, until the mixture is crumbly. Gently pat half the mixture into the pan.

In a medium bowl, stir together the lemon juice, sugar, and cornstarch. Add the blueberries, and turn them around until they are well coated. Spread over the crust in the pan, and sprinkle the remaining dough over the top. Place the pan in the oven, and bake for 50–55 minutes or until the top is lightly browned. Leave to cool in the pan completely, before cutting into squares. Store somewhere cool, in an airtight container until required.

NOW TRY THIS

apple & raspberry bars
Replace the blueberries with 3 small red apples, peeled, cored and chopped, mixed with 2 cups/9 ounces raspberries.

chocolate & caramel oat bars
Replace ¾ of the flour with ½ cup/3 ounces rolled oats. Gently press the mixture into the pan and bake for 20 minutes. Omit the blueberries. Melt 48 soft caramels with ½ cup/4 fluid ounces heavy cream. Sprinkle the base with semisweet chocolate chips and drizzle the caramel over the top. Sprinkle the remaining dough over the top and bake for 25 minutes.

cherry pie bars
Replace the blueberries with 4 cups/1 pound pitted fresh cherries. Bake as before.

kiwi & lime tart with pistachio crust

The combination of kiwi and lime is amazingly refreshing.

½ cup/3 ½ oz. finely ground pistachio nuts

½ cup/3 ½ oz. graham cracker crumbs

¼ cup/2 oz. granulated sugar

1 tbsp. lime zest

6 tbsp. unsalted butter, melted and cooled

2 large egg yolks

1 ¾ cups/14-oz. can condensed milk

½ cup/4 fl. oz. fresh lime juice

5 kiwi fruits, peeled and sliced into rounds

for the glaze

1 tbsp. fresh lime juice

1 tbsp. water

1 tbsp. granulated sugar

½ tsp. cornstarch

Serves 6

Preheat the oven to 350°F. Grease a 9-inch fluted tart pan. Combine the pistachios, graham cracker crumbs, sugar, and lime zest in a food processor. Blend in the butter until the mixture is moistened. Press the crust into the tart pan and bake for 10 minutes. Transfer to a wire rack and cool.

Beat the egg yolks, condensed milk, and lime juice until well combined. Pour into the cooled crust, and even the surface with a spatula. Bake for 15 minutes. Transfer to a wire rack. Arrange the kiwi fruit slices on top of the filling—slightly overlapping, in concentric circles.

To make the glaze, mix the lime juice, water, sugar, and cornstarch in a medium saucepan and bring to a boil over medium heat, stirring constantly until it thickens. Remove from the heat. Using a pastry brush, cover the kiwifruit slices with the glaze. Refrigerate until ready to serve, for at least 1 hour.

NOW TRY THIS

strawberry & lime tart
Replace the sliced kiwis with 2 cups/10 ounces sliced strawberries. Proceed with glazing.

raspberry & lime tart
Replace the sliced kiwis with 2 cups/10 ounces fresh raspberries. Proceed with glazing.

blueberry, kiwi & lime tart
Arrange a handful of fresh blueberries over the kiwi slices. Proceed with glazing.

mango & lime tart
Replace the kiwi slices with 2 peeled and sliced mangoes. Proceed with glazing.

chocolate-peanut butter tartlets

With peanut butter and smooth ganache, this dessert is not just for kids!

1 x 11 oz. ready-to-bake shortcrust pastry sheet

⅓ cup/3 oz. smooth peanut butter

½ cup/4 oz. cream cheese, softened

2 tbsp. unsalted butter, softened

¼ cup/2 oz. granulated sugar

½ tsp. vanilla extract

1 cup/8 fl. oz. whipping cream

¾ cup/4 oz. semisweet chocolate, finely chopped

peanut halves, to decorate

Serves 8

Preheat the oven to 425°F. Place a cookie sheet in the oven. On a lightly floured surface, use a 5-inch round cutter to cut out circles of pastry and gently press them into 4-inch individual tartlet pans with removable bottoms. Trim the excess from the edges, collect the scraps, roll out, and repeat. Cover pastry with waxed paper and baking weights, then place the tartlet pans on the hot cookie sheet. Bake blind for 5 minutes. Take out of the oven and remove the paper and weights. Lower the temperature to 350°F and bake for up to 5 minutes more, until the crust has darkened. Transfer to a wire rack to cool.

Cream the peanut butter, cream cheese, and butter using an electric mixer. Slowly add the sugar and beat until fluffy. Stir in the vanilla. In another bowl, beat half the cream until soft peaks form. Fold into the peanut butter mixture. Fill the tart shells two-thirds full with the filling. Cover with plastic wrap and chill for 2 hours.

Heat the remaining cream in a small, heavy saucepan to boiling. Pour the hot cream over the chocolate in a heatproof bowl. Stir until the chocolate has melted and the ganache is smooth. Cool for 30 minutes. Spread over the tops of the tartlets and refrigerate for 2 hours. Garnish each tartlet with a peanut half.

NOW TRY THIS

chunky peanut butter tartlets
Replace the smooth peanut butter with chunky peanut butter.

chocolate–almond butter tartlets
Replace the peanut butter with an equal quantity of almond butter.

double chocolate hazelnut tartlets
Replace the peanut butter with an equal quantity of chocolate-hazelnut spread.

chocolate chip cookie dough dip

This dip is wonderful with graham crackers, strawberries on sticks, or fresh fruit cut into slices, as it tastes as good as chocolate chip cookie dough about to be baked in the oven.

1 cup/8 oz. full fat cream cheese
½ cup/4 oz. butter
1 cup/4 oz. confectioners' sugar, sifted
¼ cup/2 oz. brown sugar
1 ½ tsp. vanilla paste or extract
¾ cup/5 oz. semisweet chocolate chips
¾ cup/5 oz. toffee bits

Serves 4–6

In the bowl of a food processor, pulse together the cream cheese and butter, until smooth. Add both sugars and the vanilla paste, and pulse again to combine.

Transfer the mixture to a medium bowl, add the chocolate chips and toffee bits, and mix until combined. Store covered in the refrigerator until required, and serve with graham crackers, pretzels, or fresh strawberries on sticks, for dipping.

NOW TRY THIS

pumpkin & chocolate chip cookie dough
Omit the toffee bits, add ½ cup/4 ounces pumpkin purée, and double the amounts of confectioners' sugar and brown sugar.

double chocolate mint cookie dough
Replace the toffee bits and with mint chocolate chips. Add ¼ cup/2 ounces milk chocolate chips to the recipe.

peanut butter & chocolate cookie dough
Replace the toffee bits with 1 cup/8 ounces peanut butter cup minis. Cut the amount of confectioners' sugar to ½ cup/2 ounces and add an extra ¼ cup/2 ounces brown sugar and 4 tablespoons creamy peanut butter to the recipe.

cordials & sodas

Cordials are sweetened, concentrated fruit syrups that you add to still or sparkling water — or for a more grown-up affair, add to sparkling apple juice, wine, or champagne. Making your own sodas means that you can create custom fizzy drinks that your group will love.

raspberry cordial

Cordials are normally made using the same amount of fruit and sugar, and this sweet and luscious raspberry cordial will have your guests begging for more.

2 ¼ cups/1 lb. 2 oz. raspberries
4 ¼ cups/1 lb. 2 oz. sugar
1 tbsp. red wine vinegar
juice of ½ lemon
soda water, to serve

Serves 6–8

Put the raspberries, sugar, vinegar, and lemon juice in a large pan and heat gently for 10 minutes until the sugar has dissolved and the raspberries softened to a pulp. Push the raspberries through a sieve into a clean bowl, add 1 ¼ cups/10 fluid ounces water, and sieve again to remove any remaining pulp.

Pour the liquid and the pulp into a medium pan and bring to a boil. Simmer for 2 minutes, pour into sterilized bottles, and seal. Store in the refrigerator for up to two weeks. To serve, pour 4 tablespoons of cordial over ice in a tall glass, and top up with soda water.

Please see page 96 for advice on sterlizing bottles and how to store homemade drinks safely.

NOW TRY THIS

black currant cordial
Replace the raspberries with black currants. Store and serve as before.

cherry cordial
Replace the raspberries with pitted cherries. Store and serve as before.

peach cordial
Replace the raspberries with peaches, pitted and chopped. Bring to a boil, simmer for 15 minutes until softened, and cool slightly. Mash the fruit to allow as much of the juice as possible to mingle with the syrup. Cool, strain, and store and serve as before.

classic lemonade

What could be better on a hot summer afternoon but a classic lemonade?
This will quench your thirst as well as remind you of childhood summers.

10 lemons (2 wax-free for zesting, if possible)

2 cups/1 lb. white sugar

1 cup/8 fl. oz. water, plus extra to dilute

Serves 6–8

Zest the 2 wax-free lemons and put into a large serving pitcher. Juice all 10 lemons, and add the juice to the lemon zest in the pitcher.

Make a simple syrup by putting the sugar and water in a large pan, over medium-high heat. Bring to a boil, stirring continuously, until the sugar has dissolved, then lower the heat slightly, and simmer for 3 minutes. Remove from heat, and pour into the serving pitcher.

Add 2 cups/1 pint cold water to dilute, and taste. If the lemonade tastes too strong, add a little more water, remembering that ice when added will dilute the lemonade further. Chill in the refrigerator for an hour before serving.

Please see page 96 for advice on sterlizing bottles and how to store homemade drinks safely.

NOW TRY THIS

cranberry lemonade
Substitute 1 cup/8 fluid ounces cranberry juice for the same amount of water when diluting.

spiked lemonade
To make one serving, place ice cubes and a few mint leaves in a tall glass, add a little bourbon, lemonade, and top with an inch of soda water.

zingy raspberry lemonade
To make one serving, place ice cubes, 2 mint leaves, and 2 tablespoons raspberry cordial (see page 84) in a tall glass, add lemonade, and top with an inch of soda water.

fizzy cream soda

This is a sweet and delicious vanilla-flavored fizzy drink made with yeast.
When chilled, it is perfect to accompany a summer picnic. It will be very
fizzy, so care is needed when opening the cap.

¼ cup/2 fl. oz. warm water

1 tsp. sugar

¼ tsp. dry active yeast

3 tbsp. sugar

2 tsp. vanilla extract

¼ tsp. cream of tartar

2-in. strip lemon peel

3 cups/1 ½ pints water

32-oz. soda bottle with screw cap

Makes 1 ½ pints

Put the warm water in a small bowl, stir in the sugar and sprinkle
the yeast on top. Set aside for 10 minutes, until frothy.

Place all the remaining ingredients in the soda bottle and shake
well to mix. Pour in the yeast liquid, replace the cap, shake and
set aside in a warm place for about 24–36 hours, no longer. Very
slowly and carefully undo the cap, and open the bottle over a sink,
as it is likely to be very fizzy. Chill for an hour or two until required,
and serve over ice.

Please see page 96 for advice on sterilizing bottles and how to
store homemade drinks safely.

NOW TRY THIS

fizzy lime & cream soda
Replace the lemon peel with lime peel.

layered italian soda
Place 2 tablespoons black currant cordial (see
page 84) in a tall glass with some ice. Slowly
add 4 tablespoons orange juice and ⅔ cup/5
fluid ounces soda water, pouring down the
inside of the glass to keep layers separated.

mango, melon & lime soda
Put 2 ½ cups/1 pint water in a pan, add
1 chopped and seeded melon, 1 chopped
mango, and 2 cups/1 pound of sugar, and bring
to a boil. Simmer 5 minutes, and set aside for
20 minutes. Strain into a serving pitcher, add
the juice of 2 limes and chill until required. Put
3 ice cubes in a tall glass, add 4 tablespoons
syrup and top with sparkling water.

peach & raspberry cocktail

A decadent champagne cocktail that looks elegant, and tastes divine.

2 ripe peaches, pitted and chopped

2 cups/8 oz. fresh raspberries, plus extra, to serve

¼ cup/2 oz. sugar

3 tbsp. brandy

1 bottle cheap Champagne or sparkling wine, chilled

Makes enough purée for 1 bottle sparkling wine

Put the peaches and raspberries into the bowl of a food processor, and pulse until smooth. Transfer to a small pan, add the sugar, and bring to a boil. Simmer for 3 minutes.

Push the fruit purée through a sieve into a medium bowl. Transfer into a sterilized bottle, add the brandy, and shake once or twice. Cap the bottle and chill for a few hours.

To serve, place one or two raspberries in the bottom of champagne flutes or tall glasses, add 2–3 teaspoons of peach and raspberry purée to each one, and top up with chilled sparkling wine.

Please see page 96 for advice on sterlizing bottles and how to store homemade drinks safely.

NOW TRY THIS

peach & raspberry soda
Replace the champagne with fizzy lemonade or soda water.

peach & raspberry cocktail with schnapps
Replace the brandy with peach schnapps.

elderfower & lime prosecco cocktail
To make one serving, place 3 ice cubes in the bottom of a wine glass, add 4 tablespoons shop-bought elderflower cordial, add a slice of lemon and 3 mint leaves, and top up with prosecco.

tropical apple fizz

To make this soda, use fruit juice that has been made not from concentrate, and you will get a gorgeous summer drink that children and adults alike will love.

¾ cup/4 oz. strawberries, hulled

1 kiwi fruit, peeled and sliced

1 ½ cups/8 oz. pineapple chunks

2 cups/1 pint tropical fruit juice

2 cups/1 pint sparkling apple juice

Serves 8

In the bowl of a food processor, place the strawberries, kiwi fruit and pineapple chunks. Pulse a few times to chop them and transfer the fruit to an airtight container. Refrigerate until required.

Divide the fruit between 8 tall glasses, add ¼ cup/2 fluid ounces of tropical fruit juice and ¼ cup/2 fluid ounces of sparkling apple juice to each glass. Serve immediately.

Please see page 96 for advice on sterilizing bottles and how to store homemade drinks safely.

NOW TRY THIS

black currant & sparkling apple
Omit the strawberries, kiwi, and pineapple chunks. Substitute 1 cup/8 fluid ounces black currant cordial (see page 84) and serve.

apricot orange fizz
Mix 1 cup/8 fluid ounces apricot juice with 6 cups/3 pints orange juice, 6 tablespoons lemon juice, and 6 cups/3 pints soda water.

chocolate soda
To make one serving, place crushed ice in a tall glass. Mix 4 tablespoons chocolate syrup with 2 teaspoons sugar, 1 tablespoon half and half, and pour into the glass. Top up with ½ cup/4 fluid ounces soda water.

cola syrup

Everyone loves an ice-cold cola, so why not try and make your own.
It's surprisingly easy and tastes just like the real thing!

grated zest of 2 oranges

grated zest of 1 lime

grated zest of 1 lemon

⅛ tsp. ground cinnamon

⅛ tsp. freshly ground nutmeg

1 section star anise pod, crushed

½ tsp. dried lavender flowers, crushed

½ tsp. minced fresh ginger root

½ tsp. vanilla paste

¼ tsp. citric acid (available from health food stores)

2 cups/1 lb. sugar

3 tbsp. dark brown sugar

soda water, to serve

Serves 8

In a large pan over a medium heat, bring 2 cups/1 pint water to a boil with the orange, lime and lemon zests, cinnamon, nutmeg, star anise, lavender, ginger, vanilla, and citric acid. Reduce the heat to low, cover the pan, and simmer gently for 20 minutes.

Place the sugars in a large bowl, and whisk together briefly. Line a sieve with a double thickness of cheesecloth and place over the bowl. Pour the contents of the pan through the sieve. Gather up the corners of the cheesecloth and twist the top to close. Use a spoon to press the bundle against the sieve, squeezing out all the liquid. Stir the syrup and set aside to cool, stirring occasionally, until the sugar dissolves. This should take about 20 minutes.

Transfer to containers and refrigerate. To make soda, pour 4 tablespoons of syrup over ice, add 1 cup/8 fluid ounces soda water, and stir.

Please see page 96 for advice on sterilizing bottles and how to store homemade drinks safely.

NOW TRY THIS

ginger syrup
Peel and grate ½ cup/4 ounces fresh ginger root. Bring 2 cups/16 fluid ounces water and 1 cup/8 ounces sugar to a boil, add ginger and 2 x 2-inch strips lemon peel, remove from heat, and set aside for 45 minutes. Strain syrup and refrigerate until required. Fill a glass with ice, add 3 tablespoons ginger syrup, 1 tablespoon lemon juice and top with soda water.

ginger, mango & melon soda
Fill a glass with ice, add 2 tablespoons ginger syrup (see above), 2 tablespoons mango and melon syrup (see page 88), and top with soda water.

cherry cola
Fill a glass with ice, add 2 tablespoons cola syrup, 2 tablespoons cherry cordial (see page 84), and top up with soda water.